HARMONY - A COLLECTION OF POEMS

ARCHISMAN PAL

Made with ♥ on the Notion Press Platform
www.notionpress.com

Contents

Contents

Preface

Hey there!

These poems are my thoughts, my emotions, and my imaginations. I've included the story behind the poem, so feel free to see those if you want a better understanding of the poem.

These poems were inspired by many things - my random thoughts, some songs, and also other random things. I started writing this book on 18th November 2022. At first these poems were a stream. That stream turned into a river, which slowly turned into a sea and then into an ocean. I hope you like my poems!

10th March,

2023.

Acknowledgements

my thanks goes out to -
firstly my mother, for being there for me and giving feedback to poems
secondly some of my friends for helping me and giving feedback
thirdly Viva Marie, a songwriter from North America, for collaborating with me on one poem
and finally I'd like to thank my teachers who have provided their guidance and helped me to write this book.
thank you!

1. Soulmate.

soulmate.

story - finding that one true person you call your soul mate

What happens when
The best thing in your life gets taken away?

What happens when
A week-old bliss ends without a way?
When the sadness takes over
And the grief erupts,
The regret will forever stay.
And emotions it will disrupt.
What happens when
Your life becomes too heavy?
What happens when
Your life is changed forever by a simple discovery?
When you memorize the date,
You know you have found,
The best thing in your life, by far,
And then it ends without a sound.
I guess we are always meant to be alone,
Forever lonely we will be.
Only if we find the perfect person,
Life will finally agree.
So the search is on,
And the lights are the best of state,
To search for that one person,
Who we call our soulmate.

2. Heartmelt.

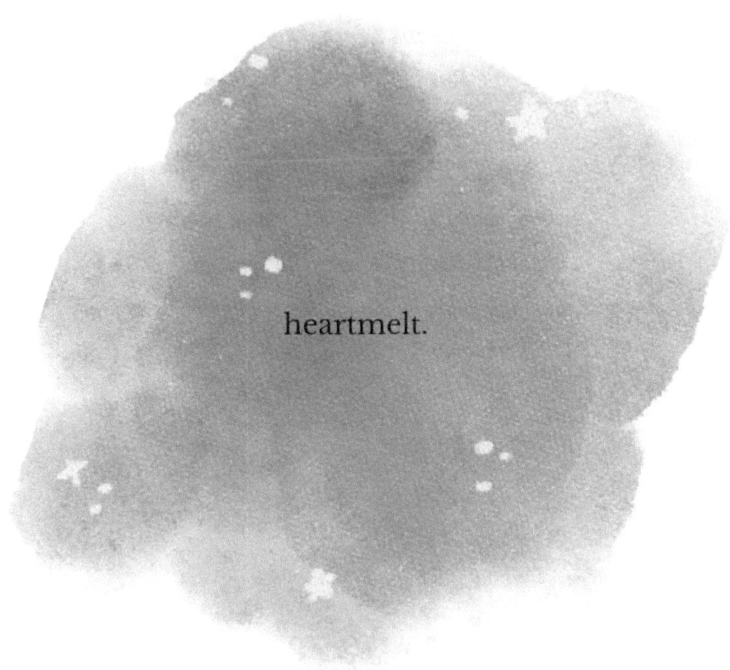

story - that urge to do everything for a special person

I could make the snows melt,
Could shine as bright as the sun.

If only everything which was dealt,
Was dealt in the one.
I could make the skies clear,
Could turn the coldest of hearts warm,
If only everything near and dear,
Were here, in this storm.
I could make the rain stop,
Make the weather sunny
But I'd only do it if,
You were here with me.
I would willingly melt your heart,
Take away all your sadness and pain,
I'll always be there for you,
And my heart forever will you contain.

3. Missing.

missing.

story - when you miss someone too much

What happens when you miss someone too much?
When you spend your whole day dreaming

And wondering what would have happened
And missing them, even when you're sleeping.
The person who made your heart beat,
Is perhaps temporarily out of reach.
Does that mean your heart stops beating?
Or does your heart start to get leeched?
That one person whom you trusted,
Is permanently gone.
You will never be able to trust someone again,
Your life will become withdrawn.
Hence, as a great mind once said,
"Hold on to the memories, they will hold on to you."
And hold on to that dearest friend,
Because a person like that, you'll find few.

4. Gloom.

gloom.

story - negativity

twin to Hope.

Why is it so, that everything which starts with something good
Ends very badly?
Why is it so, that every time you start to enjoy something,
It ends very quickly?
They say life is full of ups and downs.
Full of peaks and valleys.
But if that is true, then why is there more of the sad,
And less of the happy?
Life is just a sad pessimistic dream.
Which you just cannot awake from.
Watch it unfold just like a flower,
And slowly, you will succumb.
So enjoy the joyful times as they last,
Know that sadness is always in wait.
That single emotion which always wants to,
Leave you in the worst of state.

5. Hope.

hope.

story - positivity

twin to Gloom.

Why is it so, that everything which starts with something bad,
Turns into something good?
Why is it so, that every time you endure the hardship,
You're rewarded with something good?
Life is definitely full of mystery,
Full of uncertainties and vicissitudes.
But what triumphs over the sadness,
Is always the solicitude.
Life can be hard and unforgiving sometimes,
But you have to get through it all.
For only after you get through the challenges,
Will you confidently stand tall.
Always know that joy and grief are simultaneous,
Two sides of the same coin.
Only when you have experienced them both,
The loose ends of your life will join.

6. You and I.

story - friendship

You and I,
Struck the same chord.

You and I,

Threw sadness aboard.

You and I,

Linked by the invisible string.

You and I,

Blossoming like spring.

You and I,

Make each other happy.

You and I,

The sorrow, we carry.

You and I,

Together are unity.

You and I,

Are closer than family.

You and I,

Are best friends forever.

You and I,

Leave? We would never.

In conclusion, we are intertwined,

You and I, one of a kind.

7. Sour.

sour.

story - that one moment when everything comes crashing down, and the aftermath

The dustbin looks awfully decorated,
With my heart and all its contents.
I wonder if I'll ever be able to feel again,
After the excruciating, heartbreaking events.
I wonder if I'll be able to get back,
The useless time that I spent.
In chasing dreams which were hopeless,
And not giving my hundred percent.
Well, things do come and go,
But remembrance is forever.
Forgetting is a perpetual process,
And I will always remember.
I will always remember the date,
The year, the month, the hour.
When it all started crashing down,
And my life did sour.

8. The Honest Lies.

story - refusing to believe the truth, however positive it is

"It'll be okay again," you said,
But I refused to believe it.

I didn't know then that you actually said the truth,
And I should never have quit.
"We will be okay again," you said.
But I did not hear it.
I was too busy planning for myself,
The pain was too much to admit.
"Everything will be fine again," you said.
But I did not listen.
The sadness coursed through my veins,
And the agony did not lessen.
Your words still echo through my mind,
Every time that I think about you.
I'm all okay now, almost everything is fine,
Except right now I just don't have you.
I was dumb to not listen to you,
Because you always spoke the reality.
I should never have left you,
You were my best quality.

9. Labyrinth.

labyrinth.

story - loss of a good friendship

I've spent years building these walls,
Spent months fortifying this defense.

But you came and tore them all down,
As if all of it was just pretense.
Something clicked between us,
And the connection blossomed.
We enjoyed the time very much,
Even though we were cautioned.
Now I sit and watch those photos,
Of the good old, golden days.
And wonder what happened,
Which left me in this never ending maze.
I hope for my future,
Hope for a path back to you.
Through this endless labyrinth,
And forge a life anew.

10. Present.

PRESENT.

story - preservation of a friendship

Are we only making friends,
So that we can construct a tearful goodbye?

Are we only getting to know each other,
So we can ultimately cry?
Is friendship really forever?
Or is it ending too fast?
Does friendship really have no bounds?
Or does it never last?
Will I know you forever,
Or will you just disappear?
Will we get to live out life together,
Or will you not last this year?
The future can be tempting to think about,
Intoxicating, fascinating, and better than the past.
But the present is always more important,
So think about how to make it last.

11. Half of Your Heart.

story - being a lonely people pleaser

special inspiration from "mirrorball" - taylor swift

You spend your time making other peoples' days,
But don't figure out how to make your own.
You bide your time trying to remember the faces of your friends,
But you realize you're all alone.

Being alone is an enigmatic feeling,
Sometimes blissful, sometimes sad.
But sometimes the effect it has is,
To remember the things that you once had.
The life is yours, the choice is yours,
The whole world however is not.
Even though you feel you can take on the world alone,
You will still need someone a lot.
That someone is the person of your dreams,
That someone is the one who makes you laugh.
Out of the entirety of your heart,
You would give this person half.

12. Better Life.

better life.

story - limited friendship time

What if I told you that I was not going away?
What if I told you that I was forever going to stay?

Would you be happy? Would you be joyful?
Would you put on your smile, so beautiful?
But what if I told you that I lied to you?
What if I told you that I wasn't staying?
What if I told you that I was slowly going away,
And for my life, I was praying?
It's a hard thing, staying alive,
Made even harder day by day.
But, only with you by my side,
Can I keep the sadness at bay.
You are my hope through the darkest of days,
You are the light which keeps me awake.
Even though I may have to go away,
Till then, a better life, I'll make.

13. Nine Letters, One Word.

nine letters,
one word.

story - happiness

Nine letters, one word,
That's enough to brighten your day.

Positivity, and contentment,
Will make you figure out a way.
Nine letters, one word,
Enough to make you smile.
Your time will be spent more joyfully,
And you will be on cloud nine.
Nine letters, one word,
That will make your sadness go away.
That will make all your gray clouds blue,
And will definitely make you stay.
Nine letters, one word,
That will always not depress,
So do not worry at all,
Because that nine-letter word is happiness.

14. If I Was.

IF I
WAS.

story - the friendship in which two people stay for each other

If I was fire, then you'd be the sun,
If I was water, then you'd be the sea.

If I was glue, then fortunately,
I'd hold you very close to me.
If I was good, then you'd be the best,
If I was a picture, then you'd be the frame.
You keep surrounding me always,
And I will never forget your name.
If I was life, then you'd be the afterlife,
If I was death, then you'd be rebirth,
If I was gloom, then you'd be hope,
If I was sadness, then you'd be mirth.
If I was a lie, then you'd be the truth.
Holding me up through the highs and the lows.
If you are thankful, then I'm utterly grateful,
I always hope that our friendship grows.

15. Untrue.

untrue.

story - trusting someone painfully even though they broke it

Is it bad, that though I know what you did,
I just forgave you?

Is it bad, that even though what you did was cruel,
I'll always forgive you?
You're breaking my trust, one bit at a time,
But I think you don't really care.
If you actually did, then you wouldn't have just said sorry,
You would have made yourself aware.
I'll always keep on forgiving you,
Till the day it gets too much.
But is that day really coming?
Or is it just an idea of such?
In truth, I'm scared of losing you.
However untrue you may be.
After all, I trust you fully,
And I hope one day you'll see.
I guess it is bad that I forgive you every time,
But I have faith that you will improve.
If not, then I'll keep on trusting you,
Till the day you can over me move.

16. Salt to Your Wound.

salt to

your wound.

story - thinking that a friendship would work but in turn hurting the other person

Wasting my time on you,
Had never felt so deep.
Tonight, it feels very raw and bare,
As the sadness does creep.
How could I think we were meant to be,
When all we did was play around?
I succeeded in losing the one friend I had,
All while spinning in a snow globe, round and round.
These feelings always feel so crisp,
Feel so out of my mind, so realistic.
Nothing can really be done about them,
So I should perhaps stop being optimistic.
I hope you do know,
That it was truly all my fault.
I failed to recognize who you were,
To your wound, I added salt.

17. Know Myself.

story - with someone's help, getting to know oneself

Please don't go away,
I don't want to be alone.

Please stay here forever,
I don't want you to become unknown.
If you want to go,
Then take me with you.
Wherever you go,
I will always go too.
You can call me clingy,
I wouldn't even care.
Because, I know that, only with you,
Can I lay my heart fully bare.
You're higher than anyone,
Better than everybody else.
Only with you, did I manage to,
Get to know myself.

18. Don't.

story - false condolences

special inspiration from "bigger than the whole sky" - taylor swift

Don't say that you're sorry for me,
I know that you very well aren't.
I know that you are not even bothered,
Even though I got completely burnt.
Don't say a thing about your condolences,
When I know that you don't mean it.
If you did, then you wouldn't have just said that,
You would have helped me through it.
Don't speak about him and how good he was,
When you know I can't bear it.
You may think that that will lift me up,

But in reality, not even a bit.
Don't say that you know what I'm going through,
Because you actually, truly don't.
You can stay quiet and keep all your remarks to yourself,
And let me go through this alone.

19. Be Here For You.

story - those reassuring words of your best friend

If you feel like a mess,
I'm here to untangle you.

If you feel like a failure,
I'm here to say that that's not true.
If you feel like smashing your head against a wall,
I'm here to reassure and calm you down.
If you feel like crying yourself to sleep,
I'm here to turn you around.
If you feel like you want to die,
I'm here to make you believe.
If you feel like you're all alone,
I'm here to tell you that I won't leave.
If you feel like your insides are empty,
I'm here to fill that void up.
If you feel like wanting to criticize yourself,
I'm here to keep your hopes up.
If you feel like you could be better,
I'm here to help you through.
Because, after all, in the end,
I'll always be here for you.

20. Gravity.

story - people who want to watch you burn

You always feel proud if you achieve something,
But people are always around to demean you.

Make your achievement so small that,
You don't believe what you did is true.
People aren't always evil,
Some just want to watch you suffer.
Because of no apparent reason,
They make life for you tougher.
Ignoring them is near impossible,
Because you are always surrounded.
They are always the type of people,
Upon whom your anxiety is founded.
They say sky's the limit,
But those people are like gravity.
Always pulling you down,
And pushing you towards insanity.

21. Piece.

piece.

story - finding that lost piece of your heart

You broke your heart in two,
Searching for the perfect person.

Now you can't find the other piece,
And you yourself do worsen.
Do the perfect people really exist?
Or do we just make them up?
Can we actually find the right person to vent to,
Or is the diary our venting cup?
But yes, those people do exist,
As you realized after you endured.
For, you actually found someone,
Who you can truly call yours.
You found the other piece of your heart,
It was safely with that human.
You don't know how, but,
That person opened your life's curtains.

22. Words.

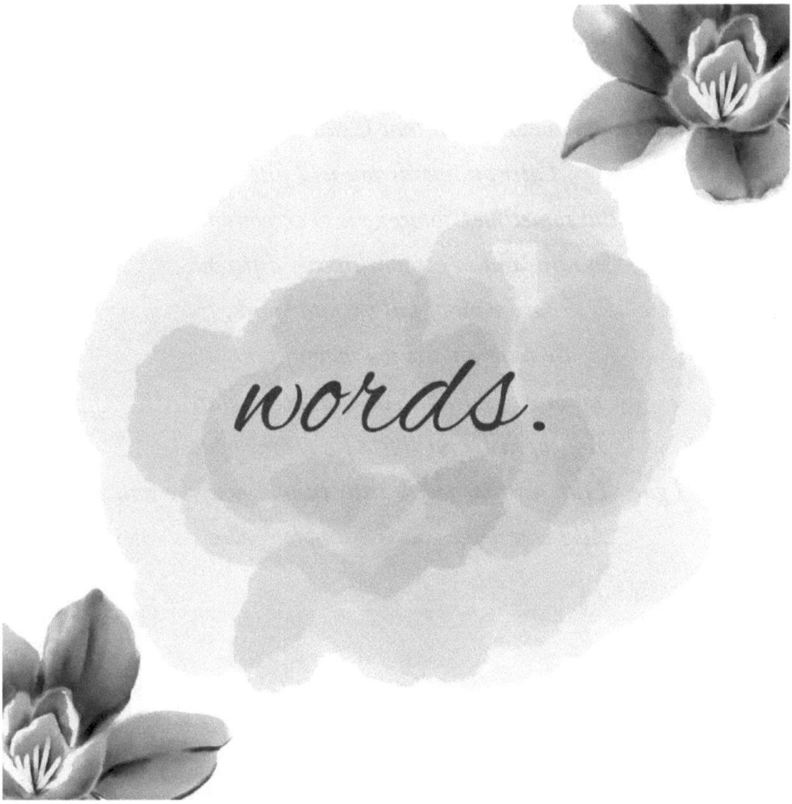

words.

story - someone so striking you have no words, except "hello!"

Words aren't enough to describe you.
But that's impossible, right?

If words cannot be used for describing,
Then it's not a description, no, not quite.
Syllables, terms and phrases,
Should get the job done.
But if they don't,
Then your options are none.
Sometimes, something is so striking and surprising,
That words leave your mind.
But that doesn't mean that it cannot be described,
Later on, words you will find.
But sometimes, someone is so exceptional,
So rare, and so extraordinarily different,
That I cannot fall back to words,
Because you are too magnificent.
You are so splendid, and so spectacular,
You captivate me like a fireworks show.
I guess I can say that words truly cannot describe you,
All I can say to you is a simple "hello.".

23. Reflecting on Love. with Viva Marie

special thanks to the awesome songwriter Viva Marie for collaborating with me on this one!

reflecting on love.

by archi and viva

story - looking back on how two people fell in love. the first paragraph is from the point of view of the boy, the second paragraph is from the point of view from the girl, and it keeps alternating.
the different paragraphs are marked by a //

We used to be classmates, but we hardly talked,
When the world shut down, we turned to each other.
I don't know about you, but the solace you provided me,
Was as if you were my own sister.
// I hadn't really seen you,
Not for who you were.
So when I think back to the old days ,
It's all just a blur.
// I guess the outcome was inevitable,
Back from the time we started talking too much.
Out of everybody else, you were the first one,
Who truly did my heart touch.
// I remember not noticing you,
But forget how we met.
And when I recall the days I didn't know you,
I only feel regret.
// We did never talk, back in those days,
We knew each other's names, but not the identity.
How would I know, that with you I'd find,
This unique type of serenity?
// The first day we talked, I remember I thought
Where have you been all my life?
And I know if you read my mind, you'd have replied,
Just two desks behind you, hoping to catch your eye.
// If I had known, that you were the one,

// I wouldn't have wasted our time.
// Because, compared to you, there really are none
// Who I can proudly call mine.

24. Future.

story - desire to go to the future

I want to go to the future,
To see what happens of me.

If I become successful, or,
If I remain dreamy.
I want to go to the future,
To see whether I get drunk,
On affection, or on pain,
And if my life ultimately sunk.
I want to go to the future,
To check upon my family.
If they made it through,
And whether they're still with me.
I want to go to the future,
To see if I started anew.
But I don't want to go,
If I see that I don't have you.

25. About to Call.

about to call.

story - the nervousness of calling a good friend after years of not talking

If I would've said that our time as friends was not good,
I'd have so clearly lied.

Even thinking about it now,
Makes me feel nostalgia in my mind.
You were my best friend,
The one through my highs and lows.
You always stayed beside me,
And always held me close.
I hope you are still the same,
And you still hold that level of affection for me.
As, I'm about to call you,
And I can't help feeling a little bit of anxiety.
I hope this is still your number,
I hope you recognize and talk to me.
If you don't, well, then,
My mind peaceful, would never be.

26. Little Things.

story - gratitude for those little things in life

I see people laughing and talking,
And wonder how I can't experience those.
I wonder how I lost that sensation,
And how the joy in my life came to a close.
Being depressed and sad,
Is not a good feeling, at all.
It takes away the happiness in life,
And makes your life seem small.
However, there are some instances,
When random people manage to make me happy.

Those are the moments when,
My life actually feels free.
Living for those little things in life,
Has never felt so good.
It gives me that unnatural feeling called happiness,
And makes me feel understood.

27. Trauma.

story - traumatic experiences

Do you really want to bring up your trauma,
In every single argument between us?

Do you really want to use your experiences,
As a way to get your supremacy in everything we discuss?
Believe it or not,
I have more trauma than you.
So much so, that,
I always try to comfort you.
Because I know what you're going through,
I know the sadness and the pain.
In helping you, you made me feel,
All those stressful emotions again.
But I don't care, because I'm there for you,
I'm always going to help you through your trauma,
Just be sure to not bring it up and use it,
As a way to cause melodrama.

28. All I Wanted.

ALL I WANTED.

story - finding happiness in another person.. and then that person leaving

As the violin starts playing,
I watch you go out the door.

I wonder if I'll ever see you again,
Or will the sadness pour.
All I wanted was to be your friend,
Yes, truly, that was all.
I did not at the least want to,
Make you feel small.
All I wanted was to be your good friend,
And for you to care for me.
I know I wouldn't have been the only one,
But I was very much able to let that concern be.
Now, I wonder if I forced you out,
With all my flaws and my dreariness.
I don't know if you will believe me now,
But all I wanted from you was happiness.

29. Tribute.

tribute.

story - tribute to the best friendship in your life

special inspiration from "invisible string" - taylor swift

We stayed together,
Through thick and thin.
We are blessed with the effect of,
The invisible string.

Connecting both of us,
And everything we hold dear.
Making sure that we are here,
For each other, and always near.
This is a tribute to us,
Our incredible friendship and absurd jokes.
With you, I finally could,
Throw away my daggers and cloaks.

I am the mystery,
Which your life unraveled.
And you are the destination,
To which I endlessly travelled.
So let us pray that we stay friends,
Till the end of time and forevermore.
If you went away, then it'd hurt,
Very much, right down to the core.

30. Come Back...

come back...

story - missing part of your life

preface - this has the same speaker as ...Be Here. in this poem, the speaker is still young

I'd drag the stars down from the sky,
So I could make a wish on those shooting stars.
I would very earnestly and truthfully pray,
To restore the life that was ours.
It was too soon for you to leave,
Too soon for me to take it.
How will I bear the weight through the years,
If I know that it is definitely going to hit?
I'd very much like you to come back,
From wherever you are.
I don't believe that you are gone,
My life, truly did you scar.
I don't know if I'll be able to get far in life,
Without your teachings and your advice.
Without you, my life feels like nothing,
It feels like I'm skating on thin ice.
So do come back, by whatever means you see fit,
And come back soon.
Because, I'll be waiting for you,
And I'll even clean your room.

31. ...Be Here.

story - that missing part of your life, but now you're grown up

special inspiration from "Come Back...Be Here" - taylor swift

preface - this poem has the same speaker as Come Back... in this poem, the speaker is grown up

If I had one wish which would definitely be granted,
It would be to bring you back here.
Because, I wanted you to see,
What happened after you disappeared.
You see, I got further in life,
Worked stronger and harder.

Now I actually am successful, but,
Never did my memory of you become shorter.
Without you, none of this would have happened,
I wouldn't even be standing where I am now.
In the short time you were with me,
You influenced my life a lot, I don't know how.
I express my utmost gratitude to you,
Express my ultimate amount of thanks.
If not for you and only you,
I wouldn't have risen in the ranks.
I've spent my time writing letters and screaming up to you,
Wondering if you could hear.
For, all I want right now from life,
Is for you to be here.

32. Through Impossible Dreams.

through impossible dreams.

story - dreaming impossible things to get through something

I want to control the sky,
I want to manipulate the stars.
I want to dream impractical dreams,
Just so I can heal my scars.
I want to feel the fire raging about me,
I want to embrace the water currents,
I want to touch the sky, and then fall back to the ground,
I don't care if it's all concurrent.
I know I dream of impossible things,
Of improbable stuff and fairytales.
But I once dreamt a lot about my life,
Before I faced my heaviest fail.
Now I dream about ridiculous stuff,
Just so I can get rid of my nightmares.
All I need to do to get everything back to normal,
Is to find a person who really cares.
I need that person who truly is good,
Who will truly have utmost faith in me.
Who will urge me on through every difficulty,
And will always, no matter what, believe in me.

33. Mother.

mother.

story - dedicated to my mother

Hi, so basically this is supposed to be,
Something resembling my utmost gratitude.

But to be honest, I really don't know how I can,
After you tolerate all my attitude.
You are a person I can fall back on,
Someone who I can always count on for help.
Someone who truly actually loves me,
And someone who I will never forget.
Please do not think I take you for granted,
Because I truly do not.
I know you still think that sometimes,
After all the times I was caught.
You should know that, yes, I do trust you,
I trust you with all my heart.
You are the one who will always be there for me,
And will always stop me from falling apart.
But I know you always will love me,
And I will love you too in return.
Because, after all, you are my mother,
You will always be of my highest concern.

34. Remembrance.

remembrance.

story - getting to be remembered

I want to be your first choice,
I want to be your definite option,

I want to be your best friend ever,
Just so I never get forgotten.
I hope you remember me,
After all that I did for you,
And also for all that I could do,
In the distant future too.
Remembrance is a funny thing,
Bringing back memories of the past.
But what we have to figure out is,
How to make those memories last.
I wish that I could be here forever,
Be here with you, that is,
Always trying to sprinkle happiness,
And never to make you miss.

35. How Are You?

how are you?

story - the false replies everyone gives to "how are you?"

When someone asks, "How are you?"
You always answer that you're good.

Nobody stands by and makes sure about it,
Well, not that they even could.
You keep yourself restricted,
Both emotionally and in your outside form.
You don't show yourself truly to anyone,
This, you cannot reform.
But when that one person asked,
"Hello, how are you?"
And you played your usual trick,
That person actually stayed for you.
That person stayed, and asked again,
And told you to answer truthfully.
That person caught on to your true self,
And held on to you with earnest honesty.
That person got you, like no one else did,
That person unraveled your identity.
You think that person was fated to meet you,
It was both of yours' destiny.

36. Closure.

story - begging for closure

special inspiration from "closure" - taylor swift

Will these feelings never end?
Will it be this hard to control my composure?
Will I get better soon,
Or will I never find closure?

I don't know about life,
It has its own needs and choices.
But I do hope that one day,
I'll be able to silence the voices.
I don't want closure, I need it,
I need a termination to the trauma right now.
I need a conclusion to this chapter in my life,
Though the process of getting that, I have no idea how.
So I'm asking you, begging you,
Please be that person for me.
Please be the person who finally provides closure,
And makes my bounds go free.

37. Karma.

story - karma is a relaxing thought-
special inspiration from "Karma" - taylor swift
What goes around, comes around,
No matter how hard you try to stop it.
Whatever you do, you have to face the outcomes,

However little you'd like to admit.
You reap what you sow,
You will always get back what you give.
Whether it be negative or positive,
Or whether it be you just trying to live.
You need to be selfish for your own good,
You need to be self-sufficient and free of others' control.
But, on the way, if you look out for others,
Your life will get completed, as a whole.
Karma always strikes back,
Whether or not you believe.
Always know, that the happiness you give,
Makes you more happy than the happiness you receive.

38. Broken Heart.

story - being guilty of destroying someone's life just by being friends with them

Am I guilty of destroying your life?
When all I did was try to be here for you?
Do I stand accused of making use of you,
When all I did was remain true?
Circumstances are strange things,
Sometimes relating to the exact opposite.
All we wanted to do was,
Make the idea of us exquisite.
All we got in return was agony,
Extreme, serious pain.
Now, I don't think I'll ever,
Be able to say your name.
We were the best of friends,
We had the time of our lives.
We were always there for each other,
And always did our sadness deprive.
I guess we were always doomed,
Always fated to break apart.
I just think we could've done it better,
So as to not leave both of us with a broken heart.

39. Risk.

risk.

story - risking it all, and then losing it all

We were so high on ourselves,
That we risked it all.

That was a huge blunder,
As we know now, after our fall.
We aimed for a life together.
And then we fell apart like a house of cards.
We had balanced it all, so carefully,
Now we will forever be scarred.
What did we do to deserve this?
Did we achieve a level of excessive happiness?
Is that even possible, or am I bringing up hypothesis,
Do I truly deserve loneliness?
I miss you. And I'll always do.
Even if we might not see each other ever again,
I'll still remember you and think of you as my best,
You were the person that kept me sane.

40. Be Like You.

story - jealousy in love

You are so confident in the way you speak,
You are so stylish, and so true.

I wish I could imitate your moves,
I wish I could be like you.
You are so studious, and so smart,
Yet you aren't socially awkward.
I wonder how you manage them all,
And how you make the lines between them blurred.
You are so happy, and so light-hearted,
Yet you manage to be pessimistic.
I wish I could own up to you,
So you could teach me how to be sarcastic.
The truth is, I want to be like you.
In every aspect of human life.
Because you are just too good in each of them,
And you make me feel alive.
I want myself to learn your qualities,
So that I have a firm trust in myself.
Then, if you ever go away from me,
My conscience can somehow prove itself.

41. Gone.

story - loss of the truest friend

My friends all left when they saw the true me,
But only you remained.

You stood by me, lifted me up,
Even though I was maimed.
I guess I should've known,
Everything in life is temporary.
Nobody will stand with you forever,
You will be alone in the cemetery.
I was mistaken in believing,
I was so confident that you'd stay.
But times changed, and you decided to leave,
I realize that today.
I thought my scars were healing,
But in reality, they deepened.
You laughed with me, made me happy,
All for it to come to a sudden end.
Now I sit down and cry,
As I play our favorite song.
Never once in my life,
Did I think that you'd be gone.

42. Loneliness.

L O N E L I N E S S .

story - loneliness. the feeling that you have no friends.

Woke up today feeling lonely,
Started the day by feeling uncertain.

But as time went on, I realized,
That I needed to draw back the curtains.
I let the sunlight in, let it flood my room,
Waited for a change to occur.
But instead, nothing happened, except,
Deep down, my sadness stirred.
Those emotions took flight,
Consumed me until there was nothing left.
All I wanted was a friend,
Now I wonder how you left me bereft.
You stole my heart, then ran away,
I never found you again.
Now there's nothing more painful,
Than the shape of your name.
You haunt me like a ghost,
It's like you never left.
Except you did, and
I admire you for your theft.
You stole my feelings, and I regret that,
You stole my mind and my thoughts.
All I wanted was you and your friendship,
But I guess you had other plots.

43. Loss of Hope.

story - when you lose hope, you lose everything. that is, if you hadn't already lost hope earlier

You had me believing in life,
But then both our beliefs were shattered.
Now you say that hope is a fickle thing,
Even though before, hope really mattered.
I was always the pessimistic one,
Always preparing for the worst.
You showed me ways I didn't even think of,
Until our lucky bubble burst.
You showed me how to trust some friends,
But they ultimately betrayed us both.
I guess now you know the mistake too,
About the consequence-filled trust growth.
Now I look out for you while you regenerate,
Although I don't get the feeling of losing hope.
Because I didn't have any to start with,
So now, we try to hopelessly cope.

44. My Best Friend.

story - that friend who will always stay for you, who will always make you happy

I was bitter winter, but you came along,
Now I'm spring, with happiness in my heart.
I was gloomy, before you came to me,
And made all my sadness depart.
I was rain, before you came along,
Now you make me shine brighter than the sun.
I thought I was too lonely to live,
But now, I might just have found the one.
I was melancholy, and feeling the blues,
But your blazing fire made my heart warm.
I was so sorrowful, so lonely and alone,
But you made me transform.
It was you I was waiting for,
The best thing I didn't know I needed.
You are the only one whom I consider my best friend,
And in making me happy, you succeeded.
I have no idea why you wanted me,
But I'm so grateful that you did.
As without you and your awesome self,
In sadness I'd always sit.

45. Forgive.

forgive.

story - knowing that you are the cause of an argument but not being able to make amends

Every time my net fluctuates,
I get nervous, my hands shake.
Because, that means one less text,
To explain what I did for this argument's sake.
I know you're very mad at me,
Right now, you're also doubting yourself.
I know, becoming friends with me was a mistake,
You shouldn't have been this close, I should've trusted myself.
I hope you know, that it was me who caused this,
I hope you know that it was not you at all, it was me.
I'm always the problem in these situations,
And now, I can only hope that you see.
I don't know if you'll forgive me,
I sincerely hope you do.
Because through all my insecurities, and my difficulties,
You are the only one who's stood true.
You help me through everything,
And now I wonder if I pulled the last string.
I hope you grant me forgiveness, yes, I do,
And I'm sincerely sorry about this whole thing.

46. You.

story - that special person

Whenever I'm sad, you make me happy,
Whenever I'm down, you help me get through.
When I'm in need of a friend, when everyone leaves me,
Only you stand tall and true.
When I need help, you're always there,
You're always here for me.
I know you'll always be that person,
Who finally sets me free.
This is me trying to do the same,
This is me trying to reciprocate.

Whenever there's an issue regarding myself,
I know you'll be gone about it straight.
Sometimes I feel lucky that I have you,
A person who truly does care for me.
A person who actually is tender and kindhearted,
To my dreams, you provided the key.
Although sometimes I feel uncertain,
If you are actually for real.
I feel like I imagined you up,
Sometimes I'm just waiting for the reveal.
But that revelation comes shortly after,
And my confidence is again restored.
As you prove yourself day by day,
And you succeed to never make me bored.
I hope I can do the same for you,
I want to make you happy and full of hope,
I want to be that friend for you,
Who always will help you cope.
I will be there for you in all your situations,
I will always be waiting for you.
I will always welcome you with happiness and joy,
And difficulties, I will always help you through.

47. Dear Life.

story - a few rightful apologies to life

Dear life, I have a few confessions to make.
However much I despise you,

However much I want to escape,
I think I have some apologies for you.
Dear life, I'm sorry for everything.
I'm sorry for hating on you,
I'm sorry for making jokes and insults,
Because ultimately, you help me power through.
Dear life, even when everyone leaves,
I know that you will stay.
I know that you will be my hope,
Through the darkest of days.
Dear life, I regret not appreciating you earlier,
Because you are my permanent ally.
Throughout my existence, you have always helped me,
Not once have you stood by.
Dear life, I hope you know,
That I appreciate and respect you.
There's a long way forward for us,
So I'll place my trust in you.

48. Twin Flame.

story - finding your twin flame

I never knew I'd find someone like you,
Never knew I'd figure life out,
I never knew anything before you came along,
Now you've left me without a doubt.
I never thought I'd be able to move forward in life,
Never thought I'd have someone by my side.
I never thought I'd be happy before you came to me,
Now you've been my life's guide.
I never expected my life to become positive,
I expected everything to crash and burn.

I never expected good things for me until you came along,
Now you've made my life turn.
I never considered the possibility of trust,
Never considered a special person in my life.
But you came along, and attained that place so easily,
And you made me feel truly alive.
You came along, and changed the course of my life,
You came along and made me realize that we're the same.
You came to me and became my best friend,
And I realized I'd found my twin flame.

49. Did You?

story - the last poem, containing references from all my previous poems :)

So, did you find the person who made your heart melt?
Did you find your friend whom you were missing too much?

Did your gloom finally turn to blissful hope?
Did you start to believe the honest lies as such?
Did you figure out the word with nine letters?
Did you start to have a better life?
Did your heart get broken, and then get fixed by karma?
Did you find someone whom you want to be like?
Did you fly through impossible dreams?
Did you successfully find that piece of your heart?
Did you finally find words for that person?
Did you realize, truly, how you are?
Did you get closure, or are you still waiting?
Did you pay tribute to your best friend?
Did somebody add salt to your wound?
Did you figure out how to not let your friendship end?
Did you get to know yourself?
Did you find your twin flame?
Were you able to be there for your friend?
Ultimately, did you find your soulmate?

Printed by Libri Plureos GmbH in Hamburg,
Germany